**The Stephen
Scarl**

presents

Larkin With Women

***a new play
by
Ben Brown***

ff

STEPHEN

JOSEPH

THEATRE

**for
Alan and Alan**

with thanks to

The British Library, The Brymor Jones Library,
Jean Hartley, Andrew Motion, The Philip Larkin
Society, Anthony and Ann Thwaite, Daniel Brown,
Jenny Brown, Jennifer Buddicom

The Stephen Joseph Theatre Scarborough

Larkin With Women
by Ben Brown

PHILIP LARKIN	Oliver Ford Davies
MONICA	Carolyn Backhouse
BETTY	Susie Blake
MAEVE	Suzy Aitchison

Director	Alan Strachan
Designer	Michael Holt
Lighting Designer	Paul Towson

Senior Stage Manager	Dawn Erica Dyson
Deputy Stage Manager	Sarah Kent
Assistant Stage Manager	Charlotte Hall

5–27 November 1999

Suzy Aitchison – Maeve

Theatre includes: *Hobson's Choice* (Stephen Joseph Theatre); *Darkness Falls* a double bill which consisted of *The Monkey's Paw* and *The Dark* (Palace Theatre, Watford); *How The Other Half Loves* (national tour); *Bedroom Farce* (Far and Middle East Tour); *A Midsummer Night's Dream, The Beaux' Stratagem* (RSC); *Last Of The Red Hot Lovers* (West Yorkshire Playhouse); *An Evening With Gary Lineker* (West End and tour); *Hay Fever* (Farnham); *The Rivals* (national tour); *Man and Superman, Daisy Pulls It Off* (West End); *Jack and The Beanstalk* (Shaw Theatre); *Mother Goose* (Theatre Royal, Windsor).

Television includes: *Absolutely Fabulous, Birds Of A Feather, Gobble, Goodnight Sweetheart, The Ten Percenters, EastEnders, Mr Bean,* three series of *The Russ Abbot Show* and two series of *Up To Something.* On radio Suzy was recently heard in the series *Love 40, New Balls Please,* and in the Miss Marple Mystery, *The Mirror Crack'd From Side To Side.* She has just finished voicing a new animated series, *The Baskervilles,* to be shown on ITV.

Carolyn Backhouse – Monica

Carolyn trained at the Webber Douglas Academy of Dramatic Art. London and West End theatre includes: Alice in *Hobson's Choice* (Lyric Theatre); Charlotte in *The Magistrate* (Savoy Theatre); *Il Combatimento Di Tancredi Y Clorinda* (Donmar Warehouse); Rowena in *A Dream of People* (RSC, Barbican); *The Beaux' Stratagem, A Midsummer Night's Dream* (RSC and national tour); *A Midsummer Night's Dream, Romeo And Juliet* (The New Shakespeare Company). Number one tours include: *Mrs Warren's Profession, Breadwinner, Richard II, Richard III,* and *Rebecca.* For the Stephen Joseph Theatre Carolyn recently played Maggie in *Hobson's Choice.* For the Chichester Festival Theatre she has appeared in *Hay Fever, Miranda, A Midsummer Night's Dream, The Human Error, Beethoven's Tenth,* and a double bill of *Educating Rita* and *Oleanna* in the Minerva Studio Theatre.

For the Salisbury Playhouse her credits include *Colombe, The Crucible, The Merchant Of Venice, Time And The Conways, Pride And Prejudice* and *French Without Tears*. For the Plymouth Theatre Royal she has appeared in *Wait Until Dark* and for the Orchard Theatre Company *Venus And Adonis*.

Television includes: *The Bill, Rides, Absent Friends, Heroes And Villains-Full Throttle, Jupiter Moon*.

Films: *Robin Hood*.

Carolyn has also worked extensively on the radio.

Susie Blake – Betty

Susie trained at LAMDA and started her career in rep at Leeds Playhouse. Theatre includes: *The Merry Wives Of Windsor, A Funny Thing Happened On The Way To The Forum* (Open Air Theatre, Regent's Park); *Kafka's Dick* (Nottingham Playhouse); *Tales My Lover Told Me, Much Revue About Nothing*, (King's Head, London); *Noël And Gertie* (Wolsey Theatre, Ipswich); *All Things Considered* (Stephen Joseph Theatre, Scarborough and Hampstead Theatre, London); *The Shakespeare Revue* (for the RSC at the Barbican, the Vaudeville and on national tour); *Under Their Hats* (King's Head, London and the English Speaking Theatre, Vienna); *A Flea In Her Ear* (Theatr Clwyd and West Yorkshire Playhouse); *Absent Friends* (West Yorkshire Playhouse and Lyric Theatre, Hammersmith); *Blithe Spirit* (Royal Exchange, Manchester); *The Double Dealer, Baby* (Library Theatre, Manchester and national tour); *Prin* (Lyric Theatre, Hammersmith and Lyric Theatre, West End); *Snoopy* (Watermill, Newbury and Duchess Theatre, London); *Tonight At 8.30* (national tour and Apollo Theatre, London); *The Rocky Horror Show* and *Godspell* (national tour).

Television includes: *Roger Roger, Sunburn, A Prince Among Men, Drop The Dead Donkey, April Fools Day, Eleven Men Against Eleven, Return To Blood River, Wake Up With..., Mud, A Year In Provence, The Darling Buds Of May, Singles, The Victoria Wood Show, Russ Abbott's Madhouse, Thank You Miss Jones, Born And Bred*.

Radio: *The Frankie Howerd Show, Week Ending, Gert And Daisy*, and *Red Peppers, Shadow Play* and *Hands Across The Sea* from Noël Coward's *Tonight At 8.30*.

Oliver Ford Davies – Philip Larkin

Oliver Ford Davies spent two years as a lecturer at Edinburgh University before embarking on an acting career in 1967, with seasons at Birmingham, Cambridge and Oxford and appearances in the West End, including *Mary Rose* with Mia Farrow. In 1975 he joined the Royal Shakespeare Company, appearing in 25 productions including: Junius Brutus in *Coriolanus*, the Banished Duke in *As You Like It* and *The Greeks*. Appearances at the Barbican have included *The Devils, Waste* and *Dr Jekyll And Mr Hyde*. From 1988-91 Oliver worked at the Royal National Theatre, where he appeared as Lionel Espy in *Racing Demon*, a role for which he received Best Actor at the 1990 Olivier Awards and played in Los Angeles in 1994. He also appeared as Player King in *Hamlet,* and in the 1993 David Hare trilogy for the RNT. Oliver's recent theatre includes: *Heartbreak House* with Paul Scofield and Vanessa Redgrave (Theatre Royal, Haymarket); *Ivanov* (Almeida Theatre and Moscow); *Naked* (Almeida Theatre and the Playhouse, London).

Oliver has worked extensively in television, where his credits include: Peter Foxcott *in Kavanagh QC, A Very British Coup, A Taste For Death, Inspector Morse, The Cloning Of Joanna May, The Absence Of War, A Dance To The Music Of Time* and the forthcoming *David Copperfield*. Films include: *Scandal, Defence Of The Realm, Paper Mask, Sense And Sensibility, Mrs Dalloway, Mrs Brown, Titanic Town* and the latest Star Wars film, *The Phantom Menace*.

Ben Brown – Writer

Theatre includes: *Four Letter Word* (Edinburgh Fringe), winner of
the Cameron Mackintosh New Writing Award 1994; *All Things
Considered* (Stephen Joseph Theatre 1996, Hampstead Theatre 1997,
Marian Street Theatre, Sydney 1998), nominated for a Writers' Guild
Best Play Award and the Barclays/TMA Best New Play Award.

Alan Strachan – Director

Alan Strachan first worked in theatre in his native Scotland as an
Assistant Stage Manager at the old Byre Theatre, St Andrews. In
1970, he was Assistant Director to Jonathan Miller on *The Tempest* at
London's Mermaid Theatre, remaining there for five years, latterly
as Associate Director. His productions there included several new
plays, revivals including Shaw's *Misalliance* and *John Bull's Other
Island* and two musical revues (which he also co-devised), *Cowardy
Custard* and *Cole*. He has directed over 20 West End productions
including *A Family And A Fortune* with Alec Guinness with whom
he co-authored *Yahoo*, in which Guinness also starred as Jonathan
Swift.

For over 10 years (1978-1988) he was Artistic Director of Greenwich
Theatre in London. He personally directed over 25 productions,
several of which transferred to the West End including: *Private Lives,
Present Laughter, Design For Living* and *A Streetcar Named Desire*.
Other credits include: *Noël and Gertie, Re:Joyce!*, which he also
directed in the USA, and several Ayckbourn plays including:
Confusions, Just Between Ourselves, How The Other Half Loves
(all in London); *Taking Steps* (New York); and *Henceforward...*
(Amsterdam). From 1991-1998 he was Artistic Director of the Theatre
of Comedy Company, for whom his London productions included:
Hay Fever, The Prime Of Miss Jean Brodie and *Loot* (Churchill
Theatre and West Yorkshire Playhouse).

His recent productions include the Touring Partnership's *Mrs
Warren's Profession* with Penelope Keith, *London Assurance* at the
Gate, Dublin and *Live And Kidding* with Maureen Lipman at the
Duchess Theatre, London. He has also directed both *Troilus and
Cressida* and *The Merry Wives Of Windsor* at the Open Air Theatre
Regent's Park. For the Stephen Joseph Theatre Alan has directed
June Moon and *Alphabetical Order*. In 1996 at the SJT he directed
Ben Brown's previous play, *All Things Considered*, which was
performed in the McCarthy auditorium, and later transferred to the
Hampstead Theatre, London. Alan has just directed *Hobson's Choice*
at the SJT.

Michael Holt – Designer

Michael has been associated with the Stephen Joseph Theatre for over 20 years.

Theatre includes: *Taking Steps, Wolf At The Door, Man Of The Moment, Time And The Conways, Othello, A Going Concern, They're Playing Our Song, Love Songs For Shopkeepers, A Doll's House, Hobson's Choice* (Stephen Joseph Theatre); *Baby On Board* (Stephen Joseph Theatre, Lawrence Batley Theatre and Harrogate Theatre); *The Woman In Black* (Stephen Joseph Theatre 1987 and 1997 and Fortune Theatre); *All Things Considered* (Stephen Joseph Theatre and Hampstead Theatre, London); *Absurd Person Singular* (Whitehall Theatre); *The Glory Of The Garden* (Duke of York's Theatre); *Rough Justice* (Apollo Theatre); Charley's Aunt (Mobil Centennial tour); *Season's Greetings* (Joyce Theatre, New York). Ballet includes: *The Sleeping Beauty, Madam Butterfly, Romeo And Juliet, Quartet* (Northern Ballet).

Opera includes: *Billy Budd, Pilgrim's Progress, La Bohème* (Royal Northern College of Music Opera Theatre); *Orlando* (Bath Festival), *Pilgrim's Progress* (Royal Opera House).

Michael's design career has taken him all over the world and includes opera productions for The Royal Opera House, Copenhagen, The Avignon Festival, The Knokke Opera Festival, Belgium, and The Brisbane Festival, Australia. He has designed a ballet production for the Hong Kong Ballet Company and numerous plays for Den Nationale Scene, Bergen, Norway and the Alley Theatre, Houston, Texas.

Paul Towson – Lighting Designer

Paul graduated from Oldham College in 1993. He worked at the Green Room, Manchester, toured with M6 Theatre Company, worked at Pleasance One for the Edinburgh Fringe and was Chief Technician at Harrogate Theatre before joining the Stephen Joseph Theatre in 1995.

Theatre lighting includes: *The Merchant Of Venice, Hot And Throbbing, Kafka's Dick, Jack And The Beanstalk, Oleanna, Bouncers, Having A Ball, The Passion Plays* (Harrogate Theatre); *Betrayal, Talking Heads, Grimm Tales, Wild Honey, Dealing With Clair, All Things Considered, Lucky Sods, Fool To Yourself, The Edge, Near Cricket St Thomas 1919, Baby On Board, Love Songs For Shopkeepers, Contacting Laura, Sweet Phoebe, A Listening Heaven, Noël And Gertie, Hobson's Choice* (Stephen Joseph Theatre); *Haunting Julia* (Stephen Joseph Theatre and national tour).

Stephen Joseph Theatre – New Writing Policy

In 1996 the Stephen Joseph Theatre Company moved to a new building with two auditoria. The Round seats an audience of 400 and the McCarthy is an endstage theatre seating 165. We aim to produce in the region of 10 plays a year, with additional late night and lunchtime shows as funding allows. The majority of our work is first productions of new plays.

When it comes to choosing plays we look for writers who have a distinctive voice, an understanding of the needs and possibilities of the stage, an awareness of audience and a strong sense of narrative. Although the theatre is associated with comedy, our interest is by no means limited to this genre.

Here at the SJT we receive a large number of scripts each week. Although it is impossible for us to comment in detail on all the plays which are submitted, we do look at each play with a view to discovering new voices we would like to develop or to hear from again.

A team of professional readers led by the theatre's Literary Manager assess all submitted material with a view to its suitability for the SJT. If it is felt that a work or writer has potential, the script will then be considered by the literary department in conjunction with Alan Ayckbourn, the Artistic Director. Should the script continue to get a favourable response, the new writer may be invited to meet with the Literary Manager in order to discuss submission, commissioning or production possibilities. Although we do occasionally produce unsolicited plays, more frequently we are looking to develop long term relationships with writers who are attuned to the possibilities of the Stephen Joseph Theatre.

The theatre participates fully in national new writing initiatives and is a regular host of the Arts Council of England's Writer in Residence scheme. A local writers' group meets weekly at the SJT and regionally we have relationships with North West Playwrights (Patron: Alan Ayckbourn), Yorkshire Playwrights and, increasingly, York University. Alan Ayckbourn also judges the International Student Playscript Competition as part of The National Student Drama Festival, held annually in Scarborough.

Photo: Adrian Gatie

STEPHEN
JOSEPH
THEATRE

Registered Charity No 253606

Yorkshire Arts

Stephen Joseph Theatre, Scarborough

Maintenance Engineer	John Vardy
Security	Coastal Security Ltd
Press and Marketing Manager	Andie Hawkes
Press and Marketing Officer	Peter Cobham
Press and Marketing Assistants*	Steven Ayckbourn, Georgina Samuels
Production Manager	Alison Fowler
Technical Stage Manager	David Lockwood
Production Assistant*	Gillian Lockwood
Senior Stage Manager	Dawn Erica Dyson
Stage Manager	Helen Reynolds
Deputy Stage Managers	Fleur Linden Beeley, Sarah Taylor Kent, Lucy McEwan
Assistant Stage Managers	Charlotte Hall, Sarah J. MacGregor
Senior Technicians	Kath Geraghty, Paul Towson
Assistant Technicians	Jessica Hodson, Paul Stear, Keir Webster
Volunteers	Peter Bevan, Tony Newton
Wardrobe Supervisor	Christine Wall
Wardrobe Assistant	Beckie May
Wardrobe Maintenance*	Katy Dove
Wigs	Felicite Gillham
Wig Dresser *	Karen Barber
Designer	Pip Leckenby
Master Carpenter	Frank Matthews
Workshop Assistant	Tony Topping
Touring/Programming	Amanda Saunders
Head Chef	James Mackenzie
Second Chef	Stuart Marsden
Assistant Chef	Paul Parker
Kitchen Assistants*	Scott Gardener, Philip Richardson, James Steel
Restaurant/Bar Managers	Kirsty Romans, Kerry Ward
Restaurant/Bar Staff	Marcus Abbotts, Sue Anderson*, Suzie Bell*, Jeremy Bond*, Lucy Lowe*, Sarah Mackenzie*, David Moor* Kath Nixon*
Shop Manager	Kate Jenkinson
Shop Assistants*	Marie Daniels, Kate Futcher, Helen Humble, Emily Thurlby

* = part time staff

Ben Brown
Larkin With Women

faber and faber

First published in 1999
by Faber and Faber Limited
3 Queen Square, London WC1N 3AU

Typeset by Country Setting, Kingsdown, Kent CT14 8ES
Printed in England by Intype London Ltd

Permission has been granted by Faber and Faber Ltd.
for the inclusion in this text of the following poems taken from
Collected Poems by Philip Larkin: 'Counting', 'I Have Started To Say',
'An Arundel Tomb', 'When We First Faced, and Touching Showed',
'Love', Sympathy in White Major, 'The Life with a Hole in it',
'Aubade' and 'Vers de Société'

A CIP record for this book
is available from the British Library

ISBN 0-571-20472-4

2 4 6 8 10 9 7 5 3 1

Characters

Philip Larkin

Monica

Maeve

Betty

Setting

*Until the last scene (and with the exception
of Scene Six), the stage is divided in two,
with Larkin's living room at home stage right
and his office at work stage left.*

*Note: where it occurs, the poetry between
the scenes should be heard in the recorded voice
of the actor playing Larkin.*

This text went to press before the opening night
and may therefore differ from the version
as performed

The intellect of man is forced to choose
Perfection of the life, or of the work

W. B. Yeats, *The Choice*

Act One

Philip Larkin's flat in Pearson Park, Hull.
'Dinah' by Louis Armstrong plays as the lights come
up on the living room.
The walls are lined with carefully shelved books and
records and there is a Black Box record player. There is
a sofa and an armchair.
Larkin, in black-rimmed glasses, a small-check, single-
breasted jacket with a pocket watch on a chain secured
to the left lapel, and orange socks, sits by the window
in the armchair with a board across his knees, reading
something with a pen in his hand. He is mid-thirties but
looks older. A tall, heavy, balding man, he looks (as he
once said) like an intellectual Eric Morecambe.
The music fades.
Pause. He's stuck. He takes a gulp of whisky.
Eventually, he leans back in his chair and calls out. His
voice is low and resonant. (According to his secretary,
Betty, women swoon when he answers the phone.)

Larkin Something meaning a sign. Two syllables. About
heraldry.

Monica, mid-thirties, appears in the doorway wearing
black-rimmed glasses and a pinny over brightly
coloured, hand-knitted, unconventional clothes. Her
blonde hair is tied back behind her fine-featured face.
She is well-spoken.

Monica How many letters?

Larkin It doesn't matter.

Monica is puzzled. Then gets it.

5

Monica Oh . . .

She thinks.

Could you give me a bit more?

Larkin hesitates.

Larkin Remember that statue we saw in Chichester Cathedral of the Earl and Countess of Arundel holding hands?

Monica Yes.

Larkin Well, that's what it's about. And it ends,

> . . . the stone fidelity
> They hardly meant has come to be
> Their final *blank* and to prove
> Our almost-instinct almost true:
> What will survive of us is love.

She thinks.

Monica . . . There is a word . . . I just can't think of it . . .

Larkin I know. The best I can do is 'emblem' but I want something with a bit more oomph.

Pause.
  Monica gives up.

Monica Sorry.

Larkin Never mind.

She thinks.

Monica What will survive of us is love . . . I like that.

Larkin Thanks.

Beat.

It's a load of crap of course. Love isn't stronger than

death just because statues hold hands for six hundred
years.

   Monica smiles.

Monica Can I read the rest of it?

Larkin Later. What's for supper?

Monica Macaroni cheese.

Larkin (*pleased*) Ah . . . (*reaching for the bottle*) Well,
mustn't eat on an empty stomach . . .

Monica Blazon.

Larkin What?

Monica Blazon.

   Satisfied, she goes out.
      Larkin thinks.

Larkin
   . . . the stone fidelity
   They hardly meant has come to be
   Their final *blazon* and to prove
   Our almost-instinct almost true:
   What will survive of us is love.

   Pause.

Yes.

   He writes it down.

SCENE TWO

Larkin's office in the library of Hull University.
   Upstage centre is a large window with net curtains.
On a table by the window is a picture of a caged gorilla
apparently screaming.

In front of the window is a very large desk. On the desk is a black phone, an intercom, and a money box in the shape of a toad.

There is a door left to his secretary's office.

Betty, his secretary, mid-thirties, arranges the post on the desk. She is tall with black horn-rimmed glasses and a 'loaf' hairstyle. She speaks with a slight Yorkshire accent.

Larkin, wearing a beige raincoat to just above the knees, enters carrying a case and a folded copy of the Daily Telegraph.

Larkin Good morning, Betty.

Betty Good morning, sir.

Larkin Have you seen this? 'Hull insured for £30,000'.

Betty is puzzled.

Just about the right price, I thought . . . But they're talking about a ship.

He puts the paper down and begins undoing the buttons of his coat.
Betty smiles tolerantly.

Betty Did you have a good weekend?

Larkin (*reflects for a moment*) Yes, I did, actually. Monica came over from Leicester.

Betty Oh yes. How's she?

Larkin Pretty well . . . Last week she gave a lecture on Macbeth, wearing tartan.

Betty smiles.

Betty Not missing you too much then . . .

Larkin smiles.

He takes his coat off, revealing a black suit and waistcoat with a watch on a chain. He hangs his coat up.

Larkin Oh, and I wrote a poem. Do you want to hear it?

Betty (*surprised*) . . . all right.

He thinks.

Larkin
Back to this dreary dump
East Riding's dirty rump
That makes me want to jump
Into the Humber.
God what a place to be
How it depresses me . . .

I'm still looking for the ending. Why does it smell so revoltingly fishy this morning?

Betty That means it's going to rain.

Larkin Ah . . .

Betty If you hate it so much, why do you stay here?

Larkin We all have to make a living . . . What's the news in the library? Any more engagements?

Betty No . . .

Larkin Or better still, disengagements? (*He laughs.*) That's the sort of news I like to hear.

Betty Actually, yes.

He stops, serious now.

Larkin What?

Betty Maeve from Periodicals. She gave him the ring back on Saturday.

Larkin Oh . . .

He's embarrassed.

Poor Maeve . . . Who was he?

Betty Just some local feller.

He sits down.

Larkin Oh well. Life goes on. Usually . . . Now, where are those plans for the new library? I'd better make sure the architects have left room for the books.

Betty smiles.

Betty I'll just get them.

She goes out.
  Larkin looks through the post on his desk.
  Suddenly, his interest is aroused by a large, bulging, brown envelope. He opens it with anticipation and smiles as he pulls out a selection of soft pornographic men's magazines.
  He begins looking through them.
  Shortly, Betty's voice on the intercom.

Robert Conquest is on the phone for you.

Larkin Ah. Put him through.

He picks up the phone and holds the phone in one hand and the magazine in the other.

Hello, Bob . . . yes I've just got them . . . well, I've hardly had time to look at them . . .

He glances through the magazine.

Yes, I like the spanking and bondage but personally I think *Bamboo* and *Frolic* are the tops. Or rather the bottoms. Send me some more of those, if you can get your hands on them.

Betty comes back in. Larkin quickly puts the porn magazine inside a literary magazine.

One moment, Betty. I'm just dealing with this poetry anthology.

Betty waits as he speaks.

(*into phone*) The corporal punishment one? (*He finds it.*) Oh yes. Well . . . I admire its painstaking realism . . . but it still leaves something to be desired. You see, you have to bear in mind that what's hidden is as important as what is revealed. (*He flicks through the pages.*) See that one on page fourteen, for instance. That's the sort of thing I'm after. All right, then? Do what you can. Bye.

He puts the phone down and looks up at Betty.

Damn thing. I wish I'd never agreed to it. And I can't decide whether to give Ted Hughes and Thom Gunn a page between them or leave them out altogether. (*He smiles.*) If you can't beat 'em, edit 'em, eh? . . . What is it then, Betty?

Betty Maeve is here.

He's surprised.

Larkin Oh . . .

Betty She'd like a quick word.

Larkin Right. Well, send her in then.

Betty goes out. Larkin puts the magazines in a drawer. Maeve, thirty-ish, appears in the doorway. She is a small, attractive woman and at this moment a little nervous.

Ah, Maeve. Nice to see you.

She shuts the door.

Take a seat.

Maeve speaks with an almost imperceptible Yorkshire accent.

Maeve Thank you.

She sits down.
He smiles at her. She smiles back.
Pause.

Larkin I was sorry to hear your news.

Maeve nods.
An awkward pause.

Anyway, what can I do for you?

Maeve Well, it's about the Library Association exam.

Larkin Yes?

Maeve Well, after what you said the other day, about taking in hand any of us that wanted to do it . . .

Larkin Yes?

Maeve . . . I've decided to have a go.

Larkin Excellent.

They smile.

Of course you do recognise it will be a lot of hard work.

Maeve Yes.

Larkin Outside normal library hours.

Maeve Of course.

Larkin smiles.

Larkin Very well . . . Well, we'll start by giving you a reading list.

He opens a drawer and rummages around.

If I can find one . . . Ah.

He pulls out a piece of paper and inspects it.
He gives it to her.

It may look rather daunting but don't worry about that.
I'll soon guide you through it. Just read the asterisked
book this week and then we'll have our first tutorial. All
right?

Maeve nods.

Larkin Now . . . (*He takes his diary out of his pocket.*)
How are you placed for Wednesday evenings?

Maeve Ah. That's a bit difficult. You see, I do my
Oxfam stint on Wednesdays. Any other day would be
fine though.

Larkin How about Thursday?

Maeve Fine.

He writes it down.

Larkin It'll be at my home. (*He hands her a slip of
paper.*) Thirty-two, Pearson Park. Top flat.

Maeve Right.

Larkin Good. I'll see you at six o'clock then.

He gets up and goes to the door. She gets up too.
He opens the door for her. They smile.

Maeve Thank you.

She walks past him.
*He closes the door, goes to the window and looks
out.*
*He picks up a tortoiseshell spy-glass from the
window sill and peers through it.*

Betty enters with the plans for the new library. She sees him and smiles.
He continues looking.

Larkin She has potential . . .

He puts the spy-glass down.

As a librarian.

Betty Ah . . .

She smiles.

Well, you know what they say . . .

Larkin What?

Betty Don't touch the female staff.

Larkin smiles.

Your plans.

She gives them to him and goes.
He sits down, spreads the plans out on his desk and begins to study them.
Pause. Gradually it begins to rain.
He looks up and smiles.

SCENE THREE

Larkin's flat.
Maeve sits alone on the sofa, nervously looking around.
Noises of tea being prepared in the kitchen.

Maeve (*calling*) Are you sure there's nothing I can do?

Larkin (*off*) No, you stay where you are. I'll be with you in a second.

Pause. Maeve waits.
  Larkin enters with a large tea tray on which are
cups and saucers, a pot of Earl Grey tea, a jug of
milk, a bowl of sugar, spoons, knives, plates, napkins,
toasted crumpets, and Gentleman's Relish. The
dominant impression is of the primrose-decorated
China tea service.
  Maeve takes it in.
  He puts the tray down on the table.

Maeve Lovely view of the park.

Larkin Yes . . . John Wain was sick there once.

Maeve John Wayne?

Larkin The writer, not the actor. We'd just come back
from a poetry reading.

  Maeve smiles.

I remember he was telling me how his work would live.

Maeve I'm sorry, I don't think I've heard of him.

  Larkin smiles.

Larkin No . . .

  He sits down.

Right.

  He sets out the cups and saucers.
  Maeve looks around the room. Sees the records and
the books.

Maeve You do have a lot of records.

Larkin Yes. Well, I get a lot of them free.

  Maeve is surprised.

I review jazz for the *Daily Telegraph*.

Maeve Oh. That's interesting. I didn't know you liked jazz.

Larkin I don't. At least not what they now call jazz. (*He passes her the paper, already open at the page.*) There's one of mine in today, actually.

He pours the tea as she reads.
She laughs.

Maeve Oh, I like this bit.

Larkin . . . Which bit's that?

Maeve (*reading*) 'There have been times recently when almost anything – the shape of a patch on the ceiling, a recipe for rhubarb jam read upside down in the paper – has seemed to me more interesting than the passionless creep of a Miles Davis trumpet solo.'

Larkin smiles.

Larkin Yes, I was rather pleased with that. Would you like a crumpet?

He offers her the plate.

Maeve Thank you.

Larkin Gentleman's Relish?

Maeve Um . . . actually, I've never tasted it.

Larkin Well, why not try some then?

She hesitates before putting some on her crumpet.
She tastes it and smiles.

Maeve Mmm.

Larkin smiles.

Larkin So, Maeve . . . tell me a bit about yourself.

Maeve hesitates.

I mean, before you came to the library.

Maeve Well . . . (*finishing her mouthful*) there's nothing much to tell really. Born in Beverley . . . went to St. Mary's High School . . . father's a dentist . . .

Larkin nods.

I told you it wasn't very exciting.

He smiles.

But I was . . .

She hesitates.

Larkin Yes?

Maeve (*shyly*) . . . Well, I was Head Girl.

Larkin (*surprised*) Really? . . . That's odd.

Maeve is offended.

Maeve Why?

Larkin No, it's just that I always seem to be coming across Head Girls.

Maeve smiles, uncertainly.
Larkin decides to move on.

And after school?

Maeve I came here to the University.

Larkin What did you study?

Maeve . . . I did a general degree in French, History and English.

Larkin Oh, I read English too.

She smiles.

Maeve I know. And you write poetry. But I didn't know you wrote novels.

He is surprised.
She indicates the bookshelf.

I couldn't help noticing them.

Larkin Well, I don't any more. I wrote those two in my early twenties.

Maeve Why did you stop?

Larkin I don't know really. But I could never write a third . . . Which was a pity. I'd hoped I was going to lead that wonderful five-hundred-words-a-day-on-the-Riviera life.

Maeve So you really wanted to be a novelist?

Larkin Yes . . . Trouble is, I don't know enough about other people. And whereas you can get away with that in poetry and just write about yourself, novels must be about other people or you're going to run out of material pretty quickly, as I did. (*He smiles.*) Oh well. ' . . . To be ambitious is to fall in love/With a particular life you haven't got/And (since love picks your opposite) won't achieve.'

Maeve Who said that?

Larkin I did.

Maeve Oh, I don't recognise it.

Larkin is surprised.
Maeve realises she has given herself away.

Larkin You know my poetry then?

Maeve . . . Only *The Less Deceived*.

Larkin That's about all there is, really. Rather a meagre output I'm afraid.

Maeve I think it's wonderful.

He is surprised again.
He smiles.

Larkin Thank you.

A tense pause.
Maeve looks around, embarrassed.
Something catches her attention.

Maeve Is that Monica?

She points to a photograph on the bookshelf.

Larkin (*surprised*) Yes.

She nods.
He is uneasy.

Maeve She's very attractive.

Larkin Yes . . .

Pause.

(*changing the subject*) Look, we'd better start the tutorial, hadn't we?

Maeve Right.

Maeve opens her bag.

Larkin So . . . Dewey's classification system . . .

The lights fade.

SCENE FOUR

Office.
The sound of building work outside.
Larkin, with a cigarette in his hand, sits at his desk staring into space.
Pause. He takes a drag.

19

Betty enters with some papers. She notes his mood but doesn't disturb him.

She goes to the filing cabinet and begins filing the papers.

Larkin You know, Betty, I cannot understand why the first thing you think of in the morning isn't death.

Betty smiles.

Betty Well, I can't understand why the first thing you think of *is* death.

She looks at him.

And I can't understand why you smoke so much either. You ought to be trying to prolong life if you fear death so much.

Larkin My father died at sixty-three and I shall do the same. If I'm lucky.

Betty Yes, you will.

Larkin looks up surprised.

Larkin What?

Betty You will because you've programmed yourself to. Mind over matter.

Larkin Thanks, Betty. I can always rely on you to cheer me up.

Betty smiles.

Betty Maybe you should do some work. It might take your mind off it.

Larkin How am I supposed to work with this going on?

The building noise continues.

Betty The rest of us seem to manage. Anyway, it's almost Christmas.

Larkin God, don't remind me. Out of the frying pan and into the fire.

Betty smiles.

Betty Are you going to your mother's again?

Larkin 'Fraid so . . . God, what an awful time of year this is! Just as one is feeling that if one can just hold on, if it just won't get any worse . . . and then all this Christmas stuff bursts upon one like a slavering Niagara of nonsense . . . And I still haven't bought any presents. Either people tell me what they want and I can't get it or they don't tell me what they want and I can't think of anything.

The noise outside increases.

Christ, I can't take any more of this.

He gets up and puts his coat on.

Betty Where are you going?

Larkin Home. See you tomorrow.

Betty Tomorrow? But aren't you coming to the party tonight?

He stops.

Larkin Oh yes. I forgot. The Christmas party . . . God, do I have to?

Betty Of course you have to. It's a party for the library staff and you're the librarian.

Larkin . . . I see what you mean. Oh well. See you tonight then.

He walks to the door.

Oh for Christmas in a lighthouse! Wouldn't it be wonderful? I wonder how one gets to be a lighthouse keeper?

He goes.
  Betty smiles, then goes over and begins clearing up his desk. She picks up a copy of the Library Association Record. *It feels heavier than it should.*
  She opens it and finds between its covers a porn magazine.
  She opens a page and looks at it, then another.
  Larkin enters.
  Surprised, Betty looks round.
  He sees what she is holding.

Larkin Ah. I see you've found my lunchtime reading . . . Not that there's much reading involved.

Betty I was just . . . tidying up your desk.

  Larkin smiles uncomfortably.

Why?

Larkin I'm a romantic. Sex is too good for the real world. Too good to share with someone else.

Betty You really think so?

Larkin No. Not really. But it's easier to come by.

  She smiles uncomfortably. Pause.
  He takes the magazine from her.

Larkin Merry Christmas.

  He goes out.
  Betty is left alone.
  Fade out.

  Fade up.
  Office. That evening.
  The sound of a Christmas party off. There is music and laughter.
  Shortly, in time to the music, Betty, Larkin and Maeve (Larkin is sandwiched between the two

*women) come dancing into the room in a conga. They
are in high spirits and have had plenty to drink.*
    *Betty picks up the photograph of Guy the Gorilla
from the desk and pretends to dance behind him and
they continue dancing round the room. Maeve picks
up the toad. Meanwhile, Larkin pulls open a filing
cabinet and takes out a bottle of whisky. The music
ends and they separate, laughing.*
    The laughter dies down.

Larkin Anyone like a drink?

He pours one into his plastic cup.

Betty No thanks . . . I think I'll get back to the party.

*She leaves.
    Larkin and Maeve are left alone.
    An awkward pause.*

Larkin Nice to get away from it for a bit.

Maeve Yes.

Larkin Actually, I'm glad to get you alone.

*Maeve isn't sure what he means by this.
    Larkin puts his hand in his jacket pocket and pulls
out a tiny parcel.*

This is for passing your exam . . .

Larkin gives Maeve the parcel.

Merry Christmas.

Maeve is thrilled.

Maeve Oh.

*She opens it.
    It's a pearl pendant.*

It's lovely. Thank you.

Larkin smiles.

Larkin There's a card too.

She finds the card and scrutinises it.

Maeve I can't read your writing. What does it say?

Larkin 'To Maeve, herself a jewel.'

Maeve blushes.

Larkin Aren't you going to put it on?

Maeve Of course.

She tries to put it on but has trouble fastening it at the back of her neck.

Would you . . . ?

He does it for her.
  Then looks at her.
  He takes her hands.
  They look into each other's eyes and smile.
  They kiss, then separate.
  Pause. Maeve looks troubled.

Larkin What's the matter?

Maeve There's something I ought to tell you.

Larkin . . . yes?

Beat.

Maeve I'm a Catholic.

Larkin smiles.

Larkin . . . right.

Maeve And I don't believe in sex before marriage.

Larkin nods, disappointed but trying not to show it.

I'm sorry but I always like to make it clear at the beginning of a relationship.

Larkin ... Very wise.

Pause.

I'm an agnostic. An Anglican agnostic.

Maeve smiles.

And I don't believe in marriage.

Maeve stops smiling.

Maeve Looks like our relationship will remain unconsummated then.

Larkin Guess so ... Pity.

Pause.

Maeve Perhaps you'll change your mind.

Larkin Perhaps. Or perhaps you'll change yours.

Maeve smiles.
Pause.

Maeve What about Monica?

Larkin What?

Maeve Well, you'll have to tell her, won't you?

Larkin looks uncomfortable. Pause.
A new dance song plays.

Larkin Oh, I like this one. Let's go and dance.

He takes her hand.
She smiles and they move towards the door.

Maeve Shouldn't you dance with someone else for a change?

Larkin I can't. You're the only person who can avoid my feet.

They go.
  The lights and music fade.

When first we faced, and touching showed
How well we knew the early moves,
Behind the moonlight and the frost,
The excitement and the gratitude,
There stood how much our meeting owed
To other meetings, other loves.

SCENE FIVE

Larkin's flat. Night.
  Larkin stands by the bookshelf flicking through a
volume of metaphysical poetry (The Metaphysical Poets,
published by Penguin in 1957).
  Maeve sits curled up on the sofa.

Larkin Ah, here he is. Andrew Marvell. The Bard of Humberside.

He comes over to the sofa.

Maeve I thought you were the Bard of Humberside.

He hesitates.

Larkin Good point. The former Bard of Humberside.

Maeve smiles.
  He sits down next to her.
  She looks over his shoulder as he reads.

'Educated at Hull Grammar School . . . he was tutor to
one of Oliver Cromwell's wards at Eton . . . protected
Milton at the Restoration . . . Member of Parliament
for Hull . . . The *Miscellaneous Poems*, 1681, were

published ostensibly by his widow, Mary Marvell, but this was some kind of legal fiction, as Marvell never married . . .' Wise man.

Maeve reacts.

Now, do you know 'To his Coy Mistress'?

Maeve (*amused*) Yes. We did it at school.

Larkin The second verse is my favourite. Shall I read it to you?

Maeve If you like.

Larkin
But at my back I always hear
Times winged Chariot hurrying near:
And yonder all before us lie
Deserts of vast Eternity.
Thy Beauty shall no more be found;
Nor, in thy marble Vault, shall sound
My echoing Song: then Worms shall try
That long preserved Virginity:
And your quaint Honour turn to dust;
And into ashes all my Lust.
The Grave's a fine and private place,
But none I think do there embrace.

Beat.

Maeve I wonder if she fell for it.

Larkin History doesn't relate. Anyway, this applies even more to you.

Maeve Why?

Larkin Well, let's face it. You're no spring chicken.

Maeve I wasn't born yesterday, if that's what you mean.

Larkin smiles.

Larkin (*changing the subject*) Oh, this is interesting. (*He reads.*) 'Marvell's father was drowned while crossing the Humber in 1641, having survived long enough to rescue his son from a brief period of Catholicism.'

Maeve Hey, what is this book?

Larkin smiles.

Larkin Do you know Herrick's, 'To virgins, to make the most of time'? 'Gather ye rosebuds while ye may'? And Donne's 'To his Mistress Going to Bed'?

Maeve Yes, thank you.

He runs his hands over her.

Larkin
Licence my roving hands, and let them go
Before, behind, between, above, below.

Maeve Philip!

She gets up and smooths her clothes.

Larkin Oh, come on, Maeve. Virginity is just an undeveloped talent.

Maeve You know my principles.

Larkin
Worms shall try
That long-preserved Virginity:
And your quaint Honour turn to dust –

Maeve Philip, why don't you believe in marriage?

He sighs.

Larkin Where do you want me to start?

Maeve reacts.

Actually, it's not so much that I don't believe in it. I'm just not cut out for it myself . . . I think of marriage as a marvellous thing for other people. Like going to the stake.

Maeve Be serious.

Larkin I am. I find it a rather morbid idea – if you do it properly. A fight to the death.

Maeve It doesn't have to be a fight.

Larkin Perhaps not. But my only experience of it was.

Maeve You were married?

Larkin No, but my parents were and they were miserable.

Pause.

And, of course, I was engaged once . . .

Maeve What?

Larkin Twice, actually. But to the same girl.

Maeve thinks.

Maeve Monica?

Larkin No. Her name was Ruth. *Is* Ruth as far as I know.

Maeve You never told me this before.

Larkin It was a long time ago.

Maeve takes it in.

Maeve Who broke it off?

Larkin I did.

Maeve On both occasions?

Larkin . . . I was confused.

Maeve Poor Ruth.

Larkin nods.

Larkin Yes.

Pause.

Maeve How did you meet her?

Larkin I was working in a library in Shropshire. It was my first job. And she was a borrower . . . She asked me if I could recommend anything, so I gave her a copy of *Lady Chatterley's Lover*. Expurgated, of course.

Maeve How old was she?

Larkin Sixteen.

Maeve Sixteen!

Larkin I was only twenty-one myself.

Maeve So she was still at school?

Larkin Yes. But she was Head Girl.

Maeve smiles.

Maeve How long did it last?

Larkin Seven years. On and off. But it was a long time ago. Anyway, the point is, I was miserable when I was engaged.

Maeve Maybe she was the wrong girl.

Larkin Maybe. But I was definitely the wrong guy.

Beat.

My father gave me two pieces of advice in life. Never get married and never believe in God. Marrying you in church would be an affront to both of them.

Maeve is upset.

Pause.

I have a confession to make. I got hold of a Catholic Marriage Service the other day.

Maeve is surprised.

Just out of curiosity. Anyway, it asks the question, 'For what purpose does marriage exist?' and answers, of course, 'Primarily for children.' OK? So . . .

Maeve You don't want children?

Larkin That's an understatement. When I was a child I thought I hated everybody, but now I realise it's just children I don't like.

Maeve . . . Why?

Larkin They're horrible, selfish, noisy, vulgar little brutes. And cruel. Especially if you have a stammer, as I did . . . No, the only reason I can see for having children is to be looked after by them in old age. But they don't even do that any more.

Maeve is depressed.
   Larkin sees this.
   Maeve looks at her watch.

Maeve I'd better go.

Larkin Right.

He helps her on with her coat.

Maeve Shall I see you next week then?

Larkin Actually . . . no.

Maeve What? Just because I won't sleep with you?

Larkin Of course not. I'm going to stay with Monica.

Maeve Oh.

Pause. Maeve is not happy.
He hesitates.

Larkin But we can still write.

Pause.

Maeve You'd better give me the address then.

Larkin Right. Yes. It's her cottage in Northumberland.

He gets a piece of pager

Here. I'll write it down for you.

He writes.
Lights fade out.

The difficult part of love
Is being selfish enough,
Is having the blind persistence
To upset an existence
Just for your own sake.
What cheek it must take.

And the unselfish side –
How can you be satisfied,
Putting someone else first
So that you come off worst?
My life is for me.
As well ignore gravity.

SCENE SIX

Monica's cottage in Haydon Bridge, Northumberland.
Larkin and Monica sit on the sofa poring over a copy
of Iris Murdoch's The Flight from the Enchanter.

Larkin *The Flight from the Enchanter.* Oh, I do love Iris'
titles.

Monica Yes, but we can't change that. It's silly enough as it is.

Larkin smiles.

Larkin You're right.

He turns the page.

Larkin 'By the same author . . . *Under the Net*' . . .

Monica *Under the Net* . . .

Larkin *Under the Net Stockings.*

Monica Yes, not bad.

Larkin No, we can do better.

Monica Or how about, *Under the Nether Garments?*

Larkin laughs.

Larkin Oh yes, put that in.

Monica writes it in.

Now, let's open a page at random.

Monica opens a page.
They read it.

Larkin Chapter. 'TEN'. We can change that for a start.

Monica Oh yes. That's much too clean. 'Ten' . . .

They think.

Larkin I've got it.

He writes it in.

I fuck my sTENographer.

She laughs. Then stops suddenly.

Monica Do you?

Larkin No . . . worse luck.

She hits him playfully.
He tosses the book aside and grips her wrist.
They wrestle with each other and he pins her down.
They stop for a moment and smile.
As they kiss, he puts his hand up her skirt to reveal
openwork stockings and red suspenders. He wears
bright orange socks.
The volume increases on some racy jazz ('I got
rhythm').
Lights fade.

The music cuts out and is replaced by a slower jazz
record ('I can't give you anything but love').

Fade up.
Larkin makes himself a gin and tonic, as we hear
his recorded voice describe.

Larkin
When I drop four cubes of ice
Chimingly in a glass, and add
Three goes of gin, a lemon slice,
And let a ten-ounce tonic void
In foaming gulps until it smothers
Everything else up to the edge,
I lift the lot in private pledge.
He devoted his life to others.

He drinks.
Monica smiles, then drinks.
He dances slowly round the room to it, a drum
stick in one hand, a gin and tonic in the other. He
occasionally sips at his drink.
Monica, lounging on the sofa, watches him.

Larkin You know, Bun, I sometimes wonder whether we
drink too much.

Monica Too much?

Larkin Oh, I don't mean for our physical health . . .

Monica What then?

Larkin We immediately float off into a sort of stylised unreality.

Monica So what? We're happy, aren't we?

Larkin Yes . . .

Monica So what's the problem?

Larkin Well, maybe that is.

Monica Being happy is the problem?

Larkin I don't want to be happy. I want to write. And happiness writes white.

Monica Not always.

Larkin Usually . . . Anyway, it's not my game.

Monica That's true. You're a moaner.

Larkin . . . I prefer to call it, in Cyril Connolly's phrase, the resonance of my despair.

Monica Exactly. A moaner. You could moan for England.

Larkin I do moan for England.

They smile.
  Pause.

Monica . . . There's more to life than writing you know.

Larkin Is there?

Monica Yes.

Pause.
   Monica has something she wants to say.

. . . I see there's a job come up in your English Department.

   Larkin freezes.

Larkin . . . Yes. Some chap retired.

Monica I was thinking I might apply for it.

   Beat.

Larkin Do you really think that's a good idea?

Monica Why not?

Larkin Well, we're swimming along quite nicely as we are, aren't we?

Monica Yes, but . . .

Larkin Well then.

Monica We could live together.

   Pause.

Larkin Bun . . .

Monica You don't want to.

Larkin No. It's not that exactly . . .

Monica What is it then?

Larkin I've said it before. I just see life more as an affair of solitude diversified by company rather than the other way round.

   Pause.

Monica OK. Forget it.

Larkin I'm sorry.

Monica No, I guessed as much. At least I know where I stand now.

Larkin I still want you to come and visit.

Pause. Monica is upset.
She goes over to her desk and takes the letter out of the drawer.

Monica By the way. This letter arrived for you.

Larkin For me?

Monica Yes.

She gives it to him.

Larkin Thank you.

He hesitates.
Then opens it and reads.
Pause.

Monica Who's it from?

Larkin Oh . . . just a colleague from the library.

Monica What colleague?

Larkin . . . Her name's Maeve . . . I've been giving her tutorials for the Library Association exam.

Monica Oh.

Pause.

What does she look like?

Larkin Small and dark.

Monica Good-looking?

Larkin No . . . Not conventionally. She's an acquired . . . taste.

He feels he's given himself away.

Monica You bastard. All this crap about wanting solitude in order to write and really you're just carrying on with another woman.

He doesn't deny it.

No wonder you don't want to live with me.

Larkin That's not why I don't want to live with you.

Monica Oh, thanks.

Larkin Look, it's nothing. We're not even sleeping together.

Monica Don't lie.

Larkin I'm not.

Monica I know you. You wouldn't have an affair and leave out the sex.

Larkin . . . It wasn't my decision.

Monica What?

Larkin . . . She's a strict Catholic.

Monica laughs.

Monica Well, thank heavens for small mercies.

She stops smiling.

Oh God.

Larkin What?

Monica She'll want to marry you then.

Larkin doesn't respond.

She does, doesn't she?

Larkin Yes.

Monica . . . Oh God.

Lights fade.

Thinking in terms of one
Is easily done –
One room, one bed, one chair,
One person there,
Makes perfect sense; one set
Of wishes can be met,
One coffin filled.

But counting up to two
Is harder to do;
For one must be denied
Before it's tried.

SCENE SEVEN

Office.
Betty arranges the post on the desk.
Larkin enters.

Larkin Listen to this, Betty. (*reading from a folded newspaper*) 'At Ilkley Literature Festival a woman shrieked and vomited during a Ted Hughes reading.' . . . I must say, I've never felt like shrieking.

Betty smiles.

Betty Did you have a good holiday?

Larkin smiles.

Larkin . . . No, Betty. I can't say I did . . . You know, I have a theory that holidays evolved from the mediaeval pilgrimage, and are essentially a kind of penance for being so happy and comfortable in one's daily life. However, even relatively speaking, this one was pretty disastrous.

Betty Why?

Larkin Monica intercepted a letter from Maeve.

Betty Ah.

Larkin My bloody fault. I shouldn't have given Maeve the address.

Betty What did it say?

Larkin Not very much actually, and I'm glad to say she didn't even read it. But that wasn't the point. She understood what it meant.

Betty Oh dear.

Larkin Yes. And then came my Freudian slip.

Betty Your what?

Larkin That night as we got into bed I happened to notice the colour of the linen so I said to Monica, 'Ah, what lovely Maeve sheets . . . '

Betty You meant mauve?

Larkin Exactly.

Betty Unfortunate.

Larkin You could say that. Anyway, to cut a long story short, the current situation is that Maeve wants to marry me and Monica wants to chuck me . . . At least she says she does . . . God, one just shouldn't be in a position like this at my age. One should have got it all sorted out twenty years ago.

Betty Do you want to marry Maeve?

Larkin A Catholic wedding in Hull? . . . I'm not sure it's really me. No thanks . . . But I don't want to give her up either . . . On the other hand, how can I abandon Monica? I mean, she's an orphan. I'm all she's got.

Betty So, what are you going to do?

Larkin . . . I don't know. I feel I want to become something other than a man. A rosebush, or some ivy perhaps. Something non-controversial.

Betty smiles.

How was your holiday?

Betty Good, thanks. I've taken up badminton.

Larkin Really? Maybe that's what I should have done . . . Oh well. I suppose we'd better get on.

He takes a letter knife and opens an envelope.

You know, Betty, I used to think I hated work but I now find it rather a comfort. One wakes up wanting to cut one's throat; one goes to work, and in fifteen minutes one wants to cut someone else's throat – complete cure!

He looks at the letter.

Oh my God . . .

He's devastated.

Betty What?

He reads on. Then looks at her with terror.

Larkin . . . It's the Vice Squad. They found my name on a mailing list of a shop they raided in Soho. They're going to prosecute me for receiving obscene material through the post.

He passes the letter to Betty who takes it and reads.

It'll ruin me. I'll lose my job. Everything.

The phone rings.
  Betty is about to answer it.

Wait a minute. It could be them.

Betty Don't be ridiculous.

Larkin It could be. Shit. What am I going to say?

Betty Why would they write *and* phone?

She's about to answer it.

Larkin Wait.

It continues ringing.

All right. You'd better answer it. But if it is them, don't say anything. All right? Say I'm out.

Betty picks up the phone.

Betty Librarian's office?

Pause.
  She gives the phone to him.

It's Robert Conquest for you.

Larkin sighs with relief.

Larkin Thank God.

He takes the phone off her.

Hello, Bob. Have they got you too? . . . Who? The Vice Squad. I've just had a letter from them. Bob, I'm finished. They're going to prosecute . . .

He stops.

What?

He listens.

You . . . bastard.

He slams the phone down.
  He looks at Betty.
  She smiles.

'Most Gentleman Don't Like Love' by Cole Porter
as the lights fade.

So the shit in the shuttered chateau
Who does his five hundred words
Then parts out the rest of the day
Between bathing, and booze and birds
Is far off as ever, but so
Is that spectacled schoolteaching sod
(Six kids, and the wife in pod,
And her parents coming to stay) . . .

SCENE EIGHT

Larkin's house in Newland Park.
The furniture is the same as before but differently
arranged.
Larkin, who now has a pink hearing aid in his right
ear, sits with a pencil and notebook, apparently in a
trance.
Pause. Monica enters with a drink and a box of
chocolates. She puts the chocolates on the table, takes
her drink and sits down.
She takes a chocolate, picks up a newspaper and
opens it.
Pause.

Larkin And so Larkin's Pearson Park period ends and
his Newland Park period commences.

Monica smiles and puts the paper down.
He puts down his pencil, gets up and pours himself
a whisky.

Yeah, well, so far I've written nothing . . . I feel like a
tortoise that has been taken out of one shell and put in
another . . . God, what a hassle . . . Abbey National

bum. Neighbours bum. Rates bum . . . Retirement bum. Pension bum. Emergency bum. Cause for concern bum. After a long illness bravely borne bum. In his day thought to be representative of bum . . . How dare they sell it over my head? After all I've done for them.

Monica They needed the money.

Larkin Sell someone else's flat then.

Monica I thought they did. Lots of people's.

Larkin Not everyone's. Writers should be housed and supported by the state.

Monica looks at him quizzically.

Well, I should be anyway.

Monica smiles to herself.

How am I supposed to work in this place? I mean, look at it. It's not exactly eloquent of the nobility of the human spirit, is it?

Monica You've made it look exactly like the other one.

Larkin But I own this one. So it's a symbol of my success . . . But my success has been built on failure. It's only as a failure that I've been a success.

Monica I know, deprivation is for you what daffodils were for Wordsworth . . .

Larkin Exactly. Possessions compromise writers. You know, someone once tried to give D. H. Lawrence a house and he turned it down.

Monica What a fool.

Larkin I disagree.

Beat.

And I hate living on the ground floor. All my poems were written on top floors.

Monica Then why don't you write upstairs?

Larkin Because that's the bedroom. All my poems were written in living rooms.

Monica Then bring the bed down here and move the living room upstairs.

Larkin Don't be absurd.

Monica shrugs.
  Pause.

Anyway, I can't think of anything to write about at the moment. I don't really want to write about myself, and everything else hardly seems worth bothering about . . . I feel like a chicken with no egg to lay.

Monica It'll come. Just give it time.

Larkin . . . Like love in a Victorian marriage?

Monica Exactly.

They smile.
  Pause.

Larkin Still, there's always drink.

He takes their glasses, goes over to the drinks table and begins refilling them.

By the way . . . for the record, I'm not seeing Maeve at the moment.

Monica hesitates.

Monica At the moment? What? You mean, for five minutes.

Larkin No. She's gone off with some Irishman. I haven't seen her for months.

Monica What about in the library?

Larkin Well, of course. But not socially. Not alone.

Monica . . . Good.

He gives her her drink and sits down with his own.
He raises his glass.

Larkin Cheers.

Monica Cheers.

They smile and drink.
Pause.
She looks at her watch.

It's getting late. I'd better get my things together.

Larkin Right. I'll give you a lift to the station.

She takes a gulp of her drink, then goes.
Lights fade.

SCENE NINE

Larkin's house.
Evening but still light.
The door opens and Larkin enters followed by Maeve.

Larkin Well . . . here it is.

Maeve (*looking around*) Very nice.

Pause.

Larkin I'm thinking of calling it The Old Mill. Everyone I know seems to live in something called The Old Mill or The Old Forge or The Old Rectory.

Maeve smiles.

Maeve When did you move in?

46

Larkin Four months ago.

Pause.

Maeve I suppose it was inevitable we'd run into each other sometime.

Larkin Yes . . . If people will keep having these parties.

Maeve smiles.

Larkin Would you like a glass of wine?

Maeve I've had quite a few already.

Larkin . . . I'm having one.

Maeve hesitates.

Maeve Oh, why not.

He smiles and goes to the drinks table.
  Maeve takes her coat off and sits down.

By the way, thank you for the copy of your book.

Larkin Oh . . . so you got it.

Maeve Yes.

Larkin I wasn't sure.

Maeve I know. I should have written but . . .

Larkin nods. He gives her the wine.

Thanks.

They toast and drink.
  Pause.

How was the launch party?

Larkin A trial. I couldn't hear a thing.

Maeve Did you go with Monica?

Larkin Yes.

Pause.

Maeve You're never going to leave her, are you?

Larkin . . . No.

Pause.

So, what do you think?

Maeve Well, there's nothing I can do about it, is there?

Larkin I meant about the book. *High Windows*.

Maeve Oh . . . Yes. I liked it.

Larkin As much as *The Whitsun Weddings*?

Maeve . . . No.

Larkin No, neither do I . . . But that was your book.

Maeve is flattered.

Maeve What do you mean?

He smiles.

Larkin . . . Yeats had Maud Gonne, I had you.

They smile, acknowledging the corn.
He takes her hand.
They stop smiling and look into each other's eyes.

God, I've missed you.

Fade out.

'I'm in the mood for love' plays.

Fade up.
Larkin's house.
Later that night.
Larkin and Maeve sit in silence.

Maeve sits alone on the sofa with her knees together looking down and very upset. She's been crying.
Long pause.

Larkin Do you want a drink?

Maeve shakes her head.
Pause.
He pours himself a whisky, sits down and sips.
Pause. Maeve has not moved.

Look, it's not the end of the world.

Maeve . . . For me it is.

Larkin Why?

Maeve Because it is. It's against everything I stand for.

Larkin We've come pretty close before. What's the difference?

Maeve Everything.

Pause.

They'll refuse me absolution.

Larkin They refused you before.

Maeve This time it's worse.

Pause.

Larkin This is the 1970s. Times have changed.

Maeve Not for the Catholic church.

Larkin Look, it's hardly a one-night stand. We've been seeing each other on and off for fifteen years. For Christ's sake you're forty-six years old! You can't be expected to hang on to it forever.

Maeve But we're not married! That's all that matters.

Pause.

I'd like to go home now.

She gets up.

Larkin (*getting up*) Right. I'll give you a lift.

Maeve No. It's all right. I'd rather walk, thanks.

Larkin . . . right.

She leaves.

'Black and Blue' plays.
Pause.
Larkin goes to the sofa and lies down on it.
He lights a cigarette.

SCENE TEN

Larkin's house.
Morning. The sun streams in through the windows.
Larkin is in the same position on the sofa.
He takes a drag on the cigarette and blows out smoke.
Betty enters wearing his dressing gown.
They look at each other. Pause.

Betty We must have had too much to drink.

Larkin Yes.

Pause.

Well, you did, anyway.

Betty You can talk.

Larkin Just like the optician's daughter.

Betty What?

Larkin Give her a couple of glasses and she makes a spectacle of herself.

Betty laughs.

Betty Well, it's not every day you build a library.

Larkin Not any more, it isn't. Thank God. But for twenty years.

Betty Yes . . .

They reflect. Pause.

Larkin Actually, I've been planning this for some time.

Betty What?

Larkin Us.

Betty smiles.

That's why I organised the dinner.

Betty I thought it was rather generous of you.

Larkin Find something to celebrate, get 'em drunk, then seduce them. That's my technique.

Betty So I've noticed.

Larkin is embarrassed. Pause.

What's the situation with Maeve? Are you still sleeping with her?

Larkin . . . Only occasionally. Her principles keep getting in the way.

Betty nods.

Betty What about Monica?

Larkin (*embarrassed*) She's rather lost interest.

Betty Oh . . .

Betty smiles to herself.

Larkin I'd have asked you sooner, only I didn't want you to think I was T. S. Eliot. He married his secretary.

Betty Oh, I know you'd never do that . . . And neither would I.

Larkin smiles with relief.

So you waited eighteen years . . .

Larkin shrugs.

Larkin I didn't want to rush into it . . . And you didn't exactly give me any encouragement. You kept saying 'Don't touch the female staff' and 'Business and pleasure don't mix'.

Betty smiles.

No one must know, though. It would compromise my position in the library.

Betty Yours? What about mine?

Larkin Right. Both of us.

Betty . . . Well, you needn't worry because I will never tell a soul.

Larkin You know, Betty. That's what I've always valued in you. Your integrity.

They smile.

God, how did I get myself into this? . . . Don Juan in Hull . . . I'd only had two women before I met you three. I'm *not* a philanderer, I'm *not* accustomed to keeping lots of girls on a string, I'm extremely faithful by nature.

Betty Casanova was a librarian.

He smiles.
Pause.

Larkin Let's go for a walk.

Betty What?

Larkin You know, drive out into the Wolds.

Betty What, now?

Larkin Well, after breakfast. Come on, get dressed.

Betty What about work?

Larkin The librarian's taking the day off. So there's not much point in your coming in, is there?

Betty What if someone saw us?

Larkin How could they? They'll be at work.

They smile and go.

'Let's Misbehave.'
    Blackout.

Act Two

Larkin's house.
Larkin reads to Maeve from a sheet of paper.

Larkin
I work all day, and get half-drunk at night.
Waking at four to soundless dark, I stare.
In time the curtain-edges will grow light.
Till then I see what's really always there:
Unresting death, a whole day nearer now,
Making all thought impossible but how
And where and when I shall myself die.
Arid interrogation: yet the dread
Of dying, and being dead,
Flashes afresh to hold and horrify.

He pauses for a second.

Maeve Lovely.

Larkin I haven't finished yet.

Maeve Oh.

Larkin That's just the first verse.

Maeve Ah. Sorry. How many more are there?

Larkin Four.

Maeve Good. It's a nice long one then. By your standards.

Larkin Do you want to hear this poem or not?

Maeve . . . Yes. Of course.

Larkin looks at her.

Larkin You don't, do you?

Maeve No.

Pause. Larkin puts the poem aside.

Larkin No. Why should you?

Maeve Sorry, it's just it's a little hard to take at the moment. What with my mother dying . . . And yours.

Larkin Right . . . Yes, I suppose people react differently.

Maeve I'm sorry.

Larkin No. I quite understand. I suppose it is a bit morbid. But I just thought I'd try it on you . . . The death-throes of a talent.

Pause.

They're publishing it in the Christmas issue of the *Times Literary Supplement*. That should put them off their turkey. But I'm not happy with it. There's always so much *more* to say . . . It's terribly unfair that one never gets any better at writing. Not like making a window frame or seducing women – (*He checks himself.*) Actually I don't get better at that either.

He smiles nervously but Maeve ignores it.

Maeve It's funny both our mothers should die in the same year, isn't it?

Larkin Yes . . . You know, mine was the same age as Thomas Hardy's mother.

Maeve Really?

Larkin Ninety-one.

Pause.

Everyone's dying at the moment. Even my doctor died the other day. Of leukaemia. He was fifty-one. You know, the University medical officer?

Maeve nods.

Imagine, knowing you have leukaemia and spending your days listening to, 'Like, I get these depressions, man,' all the time.

Maeve smiles.
Pause.

Speaking of depressions, the National Theatre is bringing *Larkinland* to Hull.

Maeve Really? But that's wonderful.

Larkin Is it? I'm not so sure. Anyway, I wondered if you'd come and hold my hand. You know how excruciating I find poetry readings. Especially of my own work.

Maeve Of course. I'd love to.

Larkin Thank you.

They smile. Maeve is delighted.

Maeve Is there a reception afterwards?

Larkin Ah . . . yes . . .

Maeve (*excited*) Oh, I'll have to think what to wear then. I'm not used to these theatrical types.

Larkin Actually . . . I'd rather you didn't come to the reception.

Maeve is stunned.

Maeve Why?

Larkin Because I don't want people to think we're together.

Maeve But everyone knows we're together.

Larkin Not officially.

Maeve looks at him hard.

Maeve Are you taking Monica?

Larkin No. She's in Leicester.

Maeve But you would take her if she wasn't?

He hesitates, caught out.

Larkin . . . yes.

Pause.

Maeve I see. So Monica's your official companion but I'm just your country mouse. Your little bit on the side.

Larkin Maeve . . .

Maeve Ashamed of me, are you?

Larkin No –

Maeve Well, have you ever considered how I might feel?

Larkin Of course I have.

Maeve (*sarcastically*) Only so you could write about it.

She takes her coat.

Well, I've had enough.

She goes to the door.

And you can stuff your bloody *Larkinland*.

She goes.
     Larkin doesn't move.

Fade to black.

SCENE TWO

Larkin's house.
Fade up on bright sunshine streaming in through the
windows.
Monica marks essays.
Larkin is in the garden.

Larkin (*off*) Hedgey! Here, Hedgey! Hedgey! Milk time,
Hedgey!

He comes back in carrying a saucer of milk.

Monica Hedgey? That doesn't seem very imaginative.

Larkin Well, what do you want me to call it? Prick?

Monica smiles.

Monica How do you know it's a boy?

Larkin smiles.

Larkin I don't . . . Anyway, there's no sign of it.

Monica Maybe it's started hibernating.

Larkin It's a bit early isn't it?

Monica Is it?

Larkin . . . God knows.

He sits down.

Sometimes I wish we were like hedgehogs and could just
roll away into a corner till the winter was over.

Monica smiles and continues marking.
Pause.

What are you marking?

Monica Essays on Tennyson.

He nods. Then smiles.

Larkin . . . How far was Tennyson's success in his own time due to the fact that he wasn't Wordsworth? Discuss, compare, contrast, illustrate. Do not write on both sides of the paper at once. Candidates preferring to be ranked by continuous assessment can get stuffed.

Monica smiles.

Monica That sort of thing.

Pause.
He looks at his watch.

Larkin Four-thirty on a Sunday. What you might call the arse-hole of the week. Lunchtime drink dead, not time for six o'clock gin.

Monica How about a cup of tea?

Larkin *Tea*? Don't make me cross.

Monica sighs.

Monica Put the telly on then?

Larkin Why, what's the point? There's nothing but chat shows and non-comedy and B-films and animals eating and/or fucking each other. And *news* – God how I hate the news. Why don't they show naked women, or pros and cons of corporal punishment in girls' schools?

Monica smiles.

Where's all this porn they talk about? I haven't seen any. All I get is sport . . . I watched England beat Scotland at netball yesterday. How my life has broadened.

Pause.

Monica You could write a poem?

Larkin Don't make me laugh.

Monica Why not?

Larkin Because I *can't*.

> *He bangs the arm of his chair.*
> *Monica is surprised at his anger.*

Larkin (*calming down*) . . . I can't do it any more. It's gone.

Monica It'll come back.

Larkin No, it won't. Not this time.

> *Pause.*

And after my in-a-funk-about-death poem, there doesn't seem much more to say.

Monica But you can't abandon poetry.

Larkin I'm not. Poetry's abandoned me. It's like going bald. There's nothing you can do about it . . . Well, I suppose I could try and fake something up, but in my experience there is really no substitute for the old irresistible urge. How did Keats put it? 'If Poetry comes not as naturally as leaves to a tree it had better not come at all' . . . On second thoughts, I'd never have written anything if I'd followed that line.

> *Pause.*

Still, I've got one more book in me. *The Brynmor Jones Library 1929–1979.*

> *Monica smiles.*

Oh well. I'd better go and mow the lawn.

> *He gets up and takes his shirt off to reveal braces over*
> *a D. H. Lawrence T-shirt.*
> *He goes out.*
> *Monica continues marking.*

We hear the sound of the lawn mower.
Shortly, however, it cuts out.

Larkin (*off*) No!

Monica jumps up and moves towards the door.
She stops as Larkin enters.
She looks at his feet but can't see anything wrong.
He looks at her, ashen-faced.

Monica What's the matter?

Larkin Dead . . . Dead . . .

Monica What is?

Larkin The hedgehog. I killed it. I left the grass too long.
I couldn't see it. Oh, why does everything have to
fucking well die?

Blackout.

I have started to say
'A quarter of a century'
Or 'thirty years back'
About my own life.

It makes me breathless.
It's like falling and recovering
In huge gesturing loops
Through an empty sky.

All that's left to happen
Is some deaths (my own included).
Their order, and their manner,
Remain to be learnt.

SCENE THREE

Larkin's house.
  Monica, wearing an eye-patch over her left eye, sits in his chair. Beside her is a table, on which are a glass of water and some pills.
  Larkin, now wearing two hearing aids, puts a rug over her legs.

Larkin There. Now, have you got everything you need?

Monica Yes, thank you.

Larkin Would you like a drink?

Monica No, thanks. I'm fine.

  Pause.

Don't worry. I won't stay for long.

Larkin Too right you won't. Soon as you're better you're on your way.

  She smiles, then winces involuntarily. She touches her eye-patch, then reaches for the pain-killers on the table beside her and takes two with a glass of water.

How bad is it?

Monica I feel I want to take my eye out, give it a good clean, and put it back again. Like a marble.

Larkin Still seeing double?

  Monica takes the patch off momentarily and squints to open her swollen eye.

Monica Yes.

  Pause. He looks at his watch.

Larkin Not long till supper.

Monica What are we having?

Larkin Macaroni cheese.

Monica Ah.

Monica smiles.
Pause.

Philip, have you taken up badminton?

Larkin freezes.

Larkin What?

Monica Badminton. Have you taken it up?

Larkin No.

Monica Has Maeve taken up badminton then?

Larkin Not that I know of.

Monica Oh.

Beat.

Do you know anyone who has then?

Larkin . . . I believe Betty plays a bit.

Monica Betty? . . . Ah . . . That explains it then.

Pause.

Larkin Explains what?

Monica Well, it's just that I found this. Under the bed.

She reaches into the pocket of her dressing gown and holds up a shuttlecock.

I believe it's called a shuttlecock . . . Rather apt in the circumstances, don't you think?

Pause. He doesn't deny it.

Larkin Bun . . .

Monica It's all right. It doesn't hurt as much second time round . . . And I can't say I blame you. Now that I'm off games.

Pause.

Is there anyone in that library you haven't slept with?

Larkin is embarrassed.
  Pause.

Larkin (*getting up*) I'll get the supper.

He goes.

'These Foolish Things' (first verse only) sung by Billie Holiday.

SCENE FOUR

Office.
  Late afternoon.
  Betty is at the filing cabinet.
  Larkin enters.

Larkin Well, thank God that's over.

Betty How was it?

Larkin Bloody awful . . . You know, it's only now that I realise how much I liked the old Vice-Chancellor.

Betty smiles.

Betty What did he say?

Larkin Well, he seemed to know far more about libraries than I liked. His first question was 'What's your payroll/

non-payroll breakdown?' I said, 'Oh, mind your own fucking business' . . . Not out loud of course.

Betty smiles.

Then he asked me how I saw the librarian's role in the University. So I explained that a librarian can be one of a number of things . . . a pure scholar, a technician, an administrator . . . or just a nice chap to have around, which is the role I like to think I fill.

Betty You didn't?

Larkin Well . . . not in quite those words. But I could feel him weighing me up for the drop . . .

Betty They can't sack you. You're a celebrity.

Larkin smiles.

Larkin Don't you believe it. I'm an anachronism . . . Now it's all computerised, I can't even issue myself a book any more.

Betty smiles.

But I won't resign. I've come this far, I might as well get my pension.

Pause.

Betty Did he say anything about the cuts?

Larkin Yes . . . Basically, he wants to know how we want to be buggered up. Like being asked which arm and which leg you want to lose. It's their idea of respecting the library and the great experience and ability of its librarian – asking first, I mean. They'll do what they bloody want, which means shrinking the library and sacking thirty people . . . So, all my achieve-ments of the last thirty years are coming undone.

They are depressed.

Oh well. Tomorrow's another day. I hope.

Larkin puts his coat on.

Betty Shall I see you this evening?

Larkin Ah . . . actually, Betty . . .

Betty Yes?

Larkin Look, I was meaning to tell you . . . Monica's developed shingles.

Betty Oh . . . I'm sorry . . . Where?

Larkin In her eye.

Betty flinches.

Yes . . . It started on Easter Saturday and she still has terrible headaches, swelling, double vision, you name it . . . So, she's staying with me for the moment.

Betty takes this in.

Betty Right.

Larkin She had nowhere else to go . . . So, I think, for the time being, we'd better . . .

Betty I understand.

Larkin . . . I knew you would.

An awkward pause. Betty continues filing.

See you tomorrow then.

Betty Yes.

He goes.
Betty stops filing for a moment and stands motionless. Then continues.

Larkin's house.
Monica, no longer wearing the eye patch, reads.
Larkin looks out of the window.

Larkin The sodding leaves are coming down again . . .
I should go and rake them up. But I can't be bothered.

Monica Perhaps they'll dry and blow away.

Larkin . . . Perhaps I'll dry and blow away.

Monica smiles.

Larkin I mean it. I'm losing weight.

Monica Why? What's wrong with you?

Larkin I don't know.

He gets up and goes over to the drinks table.

Just no appetite, tongue as dry as an autumn leaf,
general sick feeling. The usual hypochondria.

Monica Maybe you should go and see your doctor.

Larkin I have. He told me to cut down on drink. But it's
hard to see how I can cut down any further.

He pours himself a drink.

I hardly drink at all nowadays as it is . . . Gin once a
day, instead of two or three; beer at lunchtime as usual,
and a bit of cheap Spanish red to replace the gin at
supper. Perhaps a glass of port last thing . . .

He sits down again.

Monica (*smiling*) Next to nothing, then.

Larkin smiles.
Pause.

Larkin shudders.
Monica looks up.

Monica Death again?

Larkin No, actually. Mrs Thatcher.

Monica smiles.

I just keep thinking about that dinner. And not being able to join in the conversation about foreign politics. And those fatal words . . . 'But Mr Larkin, *you* haven't said anything yet.' . . . God. It doesn't bear thinking about.

Monica Then stop thinking about it.

Larkin Yes.

Pause.

You know watching her is like watching a top class tennis-player. No 'Uh-huh, well, what do other people think?' Just bang over the net . . . And she never laughed or made a joke . . . Still, at least she liked my poetry. (*He smiles.*) Guess which line she remembered? Or rather, misremembered.

Monica 'They fuck you up, your mum and dad'?

Larkin . . . No.

Monica 'Sexual intercourse began in nineteen sixty-three'?

Larkin Seriously.

Monica 'Books are a load of crap'?

Larkin 'Her mind was full of knives.'

Monica She didn't?

Larkin Her exact words.

Pause.

68

Larkin She offered me the Laureateship.

Monica What?

Larkin nods.

Larkin Says I'm the only person who can replace Betjeman.

Monica Are you going to accept it?

Larkin . . . No.

Monica is disappointed.

Monica Why not?

Larkin Because there's not much point in having a Poet Laureate who can't write poetry, is there?

Monica It's never been a bar before.

Larkin laughs.

Larkin I mean can't write at all. And to my mind a Laureate can fall silent but he cannot be dumb from the start . . . Anyway, I couldn't face being Mr Poetry.

Monica Mr Poetry?

Larkin Yes. You know, the fifty letters a day, TV show, representing-British-poetry-in-the-Poetry-Conference-at-Belgrade side of it all. And having to write poems about royal bloody babies. The only idea I've got for a royal poem is about Princess Margaret having to knock off first the booze and now the fags but I don't think that's quite what they're after.

Monica I suppose it will be Ted Hughes then.

Larkin Yes, I'll be sorry to let Ted in. The thought of being the cause of Ted Hughes being buried in Westminster Abbey is hard to live with.

Monica smiles.

Monica Oh well. It was nice to be asked.

Larkin Yes . . . It's ironic though, when I was doing good stuff no one knew or cared. Now all these compliments are paid and I can't write a line . . . Can't do much else either. All I do is turn on the spit of these awful memories.

Monica What memories?

Larkin Like that dinner with Mrs T. Nothing serious, just making a fool of myself. I have about a dozen, some as much as forty years old, and once one arrives, all the rest follow . . . Why can't I relive the good things in life? Hearing my Oxford results, having my novel accepted, passing my driving test? Has anyone ever done any work on why memories are always unhappy?

Monica They aren't. That's just you.

Larkin smiles.

Larkin Yes, you're probably right. Just universalising again. The rigor mortis of a dead poet.

Monica You're not dead yet.

Larkin Nearly. And as a poet I am.

Pause.

Monica I have lots of happy memories.

Larkin Do you?

Monica Yes.

Larkin Like what?

Monica Like when you first came to my cottage and immediately fell in love with it. You said I had a great English river drifting under my window. Like when we used to laze around, get drunk and play that game with Iris Murdoch's novels. Like when we used to make love.

Pause.

Like the holidays in Scotland or Sark. Walking and playing scrabble. And when we got our revenge on that stuffy hotel by going down to dinner in our pyjamas.

Larkin That was only you.

Monica Oh, was it?

Larkin Yes. I didn't have the guts.

Monica You had the guts to piss on England.

Larkin What?

Monica That time when we were on the Scottish border and we saw that sign saying 'England' and there was no one about so you went and pissed on it, at which point a car-load of well-born women flashed past with raised eyebrows.

Larkin I did not piss on England, I pissed *behind* England . . . England was my shield.

Monica Whatever. And then that photograph I took of you sitting demurely by it.

Larkin What I remember about that holiday is when you said how beautiful the larks sounded and I couldn't hear them and that was the first time I realised I was going deaf.

Monica smiles.
Pause.

Monica Philip, I'm feeling much better.

Larkin Good.

Monica My eye seems fine now.

Larkin Oh, that's wonderful.

Monica Yes . . . I think I'm ready to go home.

Larkin Oh . . .

Larkin considers this.

Well . . . no need to rush it.

Monica No, I'm fine. Really . . . I thought I might catch the train tomorrow morning.

Larkin Whatever you think best.

Pause.

Monica Right. I'd better go and pack then.

She gets up and goes to the door.

Larkin Bun . . .

She stops.

I don't want you to.

Monica What?

Larkin I don't want you to go.

Beat.

I'd be lonely without you . . . I'm used to you now.

Monica I'm part of the furniture, am I?

Larkin If you like. Our walking sticks hang side by side in the hall.

Monica smiles.

Only the young can be alone freely.
The time is shorter now for company,
And sitting by a lamp more often brings
Not peace, but other things.

Larkin's house.
  Monica sits alone, reading.
  The front door slams off.
  Monica looks up.
  She waits for a moment.

Monica Philip? Is that you?

  No reply.

Philip?

  Larkin enters, stops and looks at her, ashen-faced.

What's the matter?

Larkin I have a tumour in my oesophagus. It may or may not be malignant. They're going to remove it.

Monica And then you'll know?

Larkin No.

Monica What?

Larkin I don't want to know. So don't tell me, all right?

  Monica takes this in.

Monica All right.

  Long pause.

Larkin What's for supper?

  Monica is surprised.

Monica What?

Larkin I might as well eat while I still can.

Monica . . . Right. I'll go and see what there is.

Larkin Thanks.

Monica goes off left into the kitchen.
Larkin watches her go. Pause.
He goes to the phone, picks up the receiver and dials.
He waits.

(*on phone*) Hello, Betty. It's Philip here . . . Look, I won't be coming in tomorrow. I have to go into hospital for an operation . . . Yes, that's rather how I feel about it . . . Anyway, I expect Monica will want to come and see me sometime so I wondered if you might drive her . . . Thank you. That's very kind. And I'd like to see you, of course . . . Right, yes, we'll let you know. Bye.

He puts the receiver down.
He hesitates, then sits and reflects.
Pause.
Monica comes back in from the kitchen.

Monica It's on its way.

Larkin What?

Monica Supper.

Larkin Oh. Yes, good.

Monica sits down.
Pause.

Look, Bun. Suppose I've got cancer? . . . How long would you give me?
Pause.

Monica I don't know.

Larkin Take a guess.

Monica . . . Six months?

Larkin reacts.

Larkin Oh. Is that all?

He looks at her.
   She looks away.
   He looks down.

Most things may never happen: this one will,
And realisation of it rages out
In furnace-fear when we are caught without
People or drink. Courage is no good:
It means not scaring others. Being brave
Lets no one off the grave.
Death is no different whined at than withstood.

SCENE SEVEN

A hospital room.
   *Larkin, propped up in bed, watches Wimbledon on
television. We hear a rally followed by applause and the
commentator, Dan Maskell, eulogising over the exploits
of the young Boris Becker.*
   There is a chair and a bedside table.
   There is a knock at the door.

Larkin Come in.

Betty enters.

Ah, Betty.

He turns the TV down.

Betty Monica's with the consultant. I thought I'd come
on ahead.

Larkin Right . . . Well, nice to see you.

Pause.

Betty I brought you some grapes.

Larkin Great.

Betty Seedless.

Larkin Even better.

Betty Do you want one now?

Larkin Actually, eating isn't really my game any more. Now they've taken my oesophagus out.

Betty Oh . . . No. I don't suppose it would be.

She smiles. Pause.

Larkin So, what's the news from the library?

Betty I don't hear so much, now I'm retired.

Larkin Of course. How's the golf?

Betty Improving. I've got my handicap down to twenty-four.

Larkin Well done.

Little pause.

Betty I'm going to be Captain next year.

Larkin Congratulations.

Betty I shouldn't really have told you. It hasn't been announced yet.

Larkin Don't worry. I won't tell a soul.

They smile.
Pause.

You know, one of my nurses is called Thatcher.

Betty Really?

Larkin Thatcher in a nurse's uniform. Two of my fantasies rolled into one.

Betty smiles.

Trouble is, the other one's called Scargill.

Betty You're joking?

Larkin See for yourself. They wear badges.

Betty Any relation?

Larkin Thatcher isn't. I haven't dared ask Scargill.

They smile.
Pause.

So, I was right, wasn't I?

Betty About what?

Larkin About dying at sixty-three.

Betty You're not dead yet.

Larkin Nearly.

Pause.

When's Monica coming?

Betty As soon as she's seen the doctor.

Larkin Oh yes, you said.

Pause.

I want to tell her . . . .

Betty Yes?

Larkin I want to tell her that I love her.

Beat.

Betty . . . Then tell her.

Pause.
  There is a knock at the door.

Larkin Come in.

Maeve enters, with flowers.
  They are surprised.

Maeve Oh. Hello, Betty.

Betty Maeve.

Maeve Shall I . . .?

Betty No, I'll be going. He's all yours.

Maeve smiles.
  Betty kisses Larkin.

Bye.

Larkin Goodbye, Betty.

Betty I'll come again tomorrow.

Larkin . . . thank you.

She goes.
  Maeve moves into the room and gives him the flowers.

Flowers . . . lovely.

She looks around.

Maeve You don't seem to have a vase.

Larkin Don't worry. Thatcher will deal with them.

Maeve What?

Larkin The nurse. It's her name.

Maeve Oh.

She puts them aside.

Maeve sits down.

Larkin Good of you to come.

Maeve smiles.
Pause.

I'm sorry I couldn't make it to your retirement party. Though I admit I was rather dreading it.

Maeve It's quite all right.

Larkin Did Eddie read my speech all right?

Maeve Oh yes. Everyone laughed.

Larkin Good.

Pause.

Maeve How are you feeling?

Larkin Oh, as well as can be expected . . . Just killing time, really. Before it kills me. Watching Wimbledon mostly.

Maeve Oh yes?

Larkin Yes. I like that young German. Boris Becker. He's the spitting image of the young Auden. I met him once, you know.

Maeve Boris Becker?

Larkin Auden.

Maeve . . . I was joking.

Larkin Oh.

Larkin smiles.
An awkward pause.

He asked me if I liked living in Hull and I said, 'I don't suppose I'm unhappier there than I should be anywhere

else.' To which he replied, 'Naughty, naughty.' . . .
I thought that was very funny.

Maeve (*amused*) I remember when you hated Hull.

Larkin Yes . . . Well, that was when I didn't know it.

Maeve smiles.
Pause.
Maeve sees a Bible by his bed.

Maeve You're reading the Bible?

He feels caught out.

Larkin Oh . . . Yes. I gave it to myself as a birthday
present.

Maeve smiles.

Maeve . . . So? What do you think?

Larkin hesitates.

Larkin Well . . . I can honestly say, it's been a revelation.

Maeve is surprised.

I don't believe a word of it, of course, but I never
realised it was so beautifully written.

Maeve smiles.

. . . I wish I did believe it, especially the stuff about life
after death. But I don't believe anything survives death.

Pause.

Maeve Not even your poetry?

He thinks.

Larkin Well . . . time will tell.

Pause.

Maeve What about love?

Larkin What?

Maeve 'What will survive of us is love.' You said it.

Larkin Ah . . .

Larkin smiles.

Yes, the trouble with that poem is I got it almost all wrong.

Maeve How do you mean?

Larkin Well, to start with, the Earl and Countess of Arundel hadn't been like that since the middle ages. The hand-holding business was done in the nineteenth century – it was a bit of sentimental addition . . . Secondly, I've got the hands the wrong way round. When I say left I mean right and vice versa . . . And finally, someone I know said they'd visited the cathedral and been shown round by the guide, who stopped the party and said this tomb has been the subject of a poem by Philip Spender . . . So it's mistakes all along the line.

They smile.
Pause.

Look, Maeve, there's something I want to say to you . . .

Maeve waits for him to go on.
Pause.
Monica enters.
Monica and Maeve look at each other.
An awkward pause.

Ah, you haven't met, have you?

Monica and Maeve don't say anything.

Monica this is Maeve, Maeve . . . Monica.

Neither moves.
Monica keeps her hands in her coat pockets.
Pause.

Monica How do you do.

Maeve Nice to meet you.

Pause.

Well . . . I must be going . . . Goodbye, Philip.

As she is about to go, Larkin reaches out and takes her hand.
Maeve feels Monica's eyes on her from the other side of the bed and freezes.

Larkin . . . I'm sorry.

Beat.
Maeve gives an almost imperceptible nod of acknowledgement.
He lets go of her hand.
Maeve walks awkwardly past Monica and goes.
Larkin looks at Monica nervously.

Monica I've been with the consultant.

Larkin Yes.

He avoids her eyes.
She realises he doesn't want to know any more.
Pause.
Suddenly, she opens her coat and, with a flourish, produces a bottle of whisky.
Larkin smiles.

Ah. Finally, something I can use.

She smiles and pours whisky into a cup.
She gives him the cup.
He looks in.

Oh, come on. I can't even see that.

She adds a bit more and then pours one for herself.
She sits down beside him.

Cheers.

Monica Cheers.

They drink.
Larkin flinches a little. Monica is concerned.
He smiles.
Pause. A void.

Larkin Here I am then. Spiralling towards extinction . . .

Monica can't deny it.
She doesn't say anything.

Sorry. I must be brave. For the sake of others.

Monica Not for me you don't.

He smiles.
Pause.

Larkin You know, I used to hope that by writing about death I'd deal with it. That once I'd written about it I wouldn't be afraid of it any more . . . But I'm still bloody terrified.

Pause.

Do you remember when we saw that sign in the launderette: 'Dyeing done here'?

Monica tries to smile.

Monica Oh yes.

Larkin I ran away so quickly I almost got run over . . . How dangerous obsessions can be. Fear of death. Poetry . . . Wordsworth was nearly the price of me once.

Monica Wordsworth?

Larkin Yes. I was driving down the M1 on a Saturday morning – they had this poetry slot on the radio, 'Time for Verse' . . . It was a lovely summer morning and someone suddenly started reading the Immortality Ode, and I couldn't see for tears. And when you're driving down the middle lane at seventy miles an hour . . . It's amazing how effective it was when one was totally unprepared for it.

Pause.

Still, there's more to life than poetry . . .

He reflects.

You used to say that . . . I disagreed with you at the time. But not any more. There's nothing to write which is better than life itself . . . No matter how it might let you down, or pass you by.

Pause.

If there is an after-life maybe I'll meet Wordsworth there. Or Hardy. I'd like to meet Hardy. If you could meet any poet who would you choose?

Monica You.

Larkin smiles.
  He takes her hand. Pause.

Larkin I've been lucky. On the whole, people have treated me better than I've treated them. Especially you.

Monica Oh well. I guess you must have some redeeming qualities . . . Otherwise we wouldn't stick by you, would we?

He smiles weakly.
  Pause.

Monica looks at her watch.

Monica It's chucking out time. I'd better go.

Larkin nods.
Monica kisses him.
He holds on to her hand.

Larkin I love you, Bun.

He keeps her hand.

Remember that, won't you?

Pause. She smiles.
He lets it go.

Monica See you tomorrow.

Larkin hesitates.

Larkin . . . yes.

She goes, leaving Larkin alone.
Pause.

'I Can't Give You Anything but Love' plays.

As the lights fade, Larkin lies back on the bed and closes his eyes.
Monica, Maeve and Betty enter from different sides of the stage and stand over him, Monica at the top of the bed, Maeve and Betty at the foot.
The lights fade to black.

Discover the brightest and best in fresh theatre writing
with Faber's new StageScripts